A Paines Plough P

The Human Ear

by Alexandra Wood

The first performance of *The Human Ear* took place on
6 August 2015 in Paines Plough's Roundabout
at Summerhall, Edinburgh.

Paines
Plough

Supported by
ARTS COUNCIL
ENGLAND

The Human Ear

by Alexandra Wood

Cast

Lucy	Sian Reese-Williams
Man/Ed	Abdul Salis

Creative Team

Direction	George Perrin
Lighting Design	Emma Chapman
Sound Design	Dominic Kennedy
Producer	Hanna Streeter
Assistant Producer	Francesca Moody
Company Stage Manager	Sarah Thomas
Technical Stage Manager	James Ball

ALEXANDRA WOOD (Playwright)
Alexandra's plays include *The Initiate* (Paines Plough, Scotsman Fringe First); *Ages* (Old Vic New Voices); an English version of Manfred Karge's *Man to Man* (Wales Millennium Centre); *Merit* (Theatre Royal Plymouth); *The Empty Quarter* (Hampstead); an adaptation of Jung Chang's *Wild Swans* (Young Vic); *The Centre* (Islington Community Theatre); *Decade* (co-writer, Headlong); *Unbroken* (Gate); *The Lion's Mouth* (Royal Court Rough Cuts); *The Eleventh Capital* (Royal Court) and the radio play *Twelve Years* (BBC Radio 4). She is a winner of the George Devine Award and was the Big Room playwright-in-residence at Paines Plough in 2013.

SIAN REESE-WILLIAMS (Lucy)
Theatre credits include: *Lungs*, *The Initiate*, *Our Teacher's A Troll* (Paines Plough); *Enjoy* (West Yorkshire Playhouse); *Children of Fate* (Bussey Building); *Be My Baby* (New Vic); *As You Like It* (Derby Playhouse); *The Future Perfect* season (Paines Plough/Rose Bruford); *Coltan* (Paines Plough), *Sixty Five Miles* (Paines Plough/Hull Truck); *Diamond* (King's Head); *The Dreaming* (National Youth Music Theatre); *Into the Woods* (National Youth Music Theatre).

TV credits include: *Emmerdale* (ITV) and *Cowbois Ac Injians* (Opus Tf).

ABDUL SALIS (Man/Ed)
Theatre credits include: *Lungs*, *The Initiate*, *Our Teacher's A Troll* (Paines Plough); *The Rise and Shine of Comrade Fiasco* (Paul Jellis/Gate); *Joe Guy* (Tiata Fahodzi); *Exonnerated*, *War Horse* (National Theatre); *Don Juan in Soho* (Donmar Warehouse); *Henry V* (Unicorn).

TV credits include: *Doctors* (Blunt Pictures); *Hacks, Outnumbered, Trevor's World of Sport* (Hat Trick Productions); *Strike Back* (Left Bank Pictures); *Victoria Wood Christmas Special* (Phil McIntyre Productions); *Casualty* (BBC); *M.I. High* (Kudos For BBC); *The Bill* (Talkback Thames); *Doctor Who* (BBC/DW Productions); *Gifted* (Red Productions); *Roger Roger* (BBC); *The Hidden City* (Hallmark Entertainment).

Film credits include: *Fly Boys* (Electric Entertainments); *Animal* (Animal Productions); *Sahara* (Sahara Productions); *Welcome Home* (Wega-Film); *Love, Actually* (DNA/Working Title).

Radio includes: *Skyvers* (BBC Radio 3)

GEORGE PERRIN (Direction)
George Perrin is the joint Artistic Director of Paines Plough. He was formerly co-founder and Joint Artistic Director of nabokov and Trainee Associate Director at Paines Plough and Watford Palace Theatre.

Directing credits for Paines Plough include *Every Brilliant Thing* by Duncan Macmillan with Jonny Donahoe, *The Initiate* by Alexandra Wood, *Lungs* by Duncan Macmillan, *Our Teacher's A Troll* by Dennis Kelly (Roundabout Season, Edinburgh Festival Fringe and national tour); *Not The Worst Place* by Sam Burns (Sherman Cymru, Theatr Clwyd); *Sea Wall* by Simon Stephens (Project Arts Centre, Dublin/National Theatre Shed); *Good With People* by David Harrower (59East59 Theatres New York/Traverse/Orán Mòr); *London* by Simon Stephens (national tour); *Sixty Five Miles* by Matt Hartley (Hull Truck); *The 8th* by Che Walker and Paul Heaton (Latitude Festival/Barbican/Manchester International Festival/national tour); *Dig* by Katie Douglas and *Juicy Fruits* by Leo Butler (Orán Mòr/national tour) .

As Trainee Associate Director of Paines Plough, directing credits include *House Of Agnes* by Levi David Addai; *The Dirt Under the Carpet* by Rona Munro; *Crazy Love* by Che Walker; *My Little Heart Dropped In Coffee* by Duncan Macmillan and *Babies* by Katie Douglas.

Further directing credits include *2nd May 1997* by Jack Thorne (Bush); *Terre Haute* by Edmund White (59East59 Theatres New York/West End/national tour/Assembly Rooms, Edinburgh Festival Fringe); *Is Everyone OK?* and *Public Displays Of Affection* by Joel Horwood and *Camarilla* by Van Badham (nabokov).

EMMA CHAPMAN (Lighting Design)

Emma Chapman trained at Bristol Old Vic Theatre School.

With Lucy Osborne and Howard Eaton, Emma Chapman designed The Stage Awards' Theatre Building of the Year 2015: Roundabout, commissioned by Paines Plough.

Theatre credits include: a co-production between Watford Palace Theatre and West Yorkshire Playhouse of *Boi Boi is Dead*; *Lungs*, *The Initiate*, *Our Teacher's A Troll* (Roundabout, Paines Plough); *Rose* (Edinburgh); *The Planet and Stuff*, *Run*, *The Machine Gunners* (Polka); *Dublin Carol* (Donmar season); *Sex with a Stranger* (Trafalgar Studios); *The Sea Plays* (Old Vic Tunnels); *Donkey's Years* (Rose, Kingston); *Mules*, *You Can See the Hills*, *Parallel Hamlet* (Young Vic); *Bus Stop* (New Vic, Stoke/Stephen Joseph Theatre); *Dangerous Corner*, *Dick Whittington* (Theatre Royal, Bury St Edmunds); *Lulu* (Gate).

Opera credits include *Xerxes*, *Carmen* (Royal Northern College of Music, Manchester); *Così fan tutte* (Royal College of Music); *The Pied Piper* (Opera North) and *Il Turco In Italia* (Angers/Nantes Opera an Luxembourg).

She has also lit *Rumplestiltskin* for London Children's Ballet at the Peacock Theatre, available on DVD.

Other notable engagements include Olivier Award-winning play *The Mountaintop* (Theatre503/Trafalgar Studio); *The Painter*, which opened the new Arcola Theatre; *Wet Weather Cover* (King's Head/Arts Theatre).

DOMINIC KENNEDY (Sound Design)

Dominic Kennedy is a Sound Designer and Composer for performance and live events; he has a keen interest in developing new work and implementing Sound Design at an early stage of a process. Dominic is a graduate from RCSSD where he developed specialist skills in collaborative and devised theatre-making. Dominic has worked as an Associate Sound Designer with Tom Gibbons on a number of Paines Plough productions including *Lungs*, *The Initiate*, *Hopelessly Devoted*, and *The Angry Brigade*; he also composed original music for *Our Teacher's A Troll*. Recent Sound Design credits include *This Much (or An Act of Violence Towards the Institution of Marriage)* (Moving Dust); *With A Little Bit Of Luck* (Paines Plough/Latitude); *Crocodiles* at the Manchester Royal Exchange; *Ono* at Ovalhouse; *This Is The Moon* at The Yard; *Run* at the New Diorama.

The national theatre of new plays

Paines Plough

'Revered touring company Paines Plough' *Time Out*

Paines Plough is the UK's national theatre of new plays. We commission and produce the best playwrights and tour their plays far and wide. Whether you're in Liverpool or Lyme Regis, Scarborough or Southampton, a Paines Plough show is coming to a theatre near you soon.

'The lifeblood of the UK's theatre ecosystem' *Guardian*

Paines Plough was formed in 1974 over a pint of Paines bitter in the Plough pub. Since then we've produced more than 150 new productions by world-renowned playwrights like Stephen Jeffreys, Abi Morgan, Sarah Kane, Mark Ravenhill, Dennis Kelly and Mike Bartlett. We've toured those plays to hundreds of places from Manchester to Moscow to Maidenhead.

'That noble company Paines Plough, de facto national theatre of new writing' *Telegraph*

Our Programme 2015 sees 11 productions by the nation's finest writers touring to 74 places from Cornwall to the Orkney Islands; in village halls and Off-Broadway, at music festivals and student unions, online and on radio, and in our own pop-up theatre Roundabout.

'I think some theatre just saved my life' @kate_clement on Twitter

Welcome to Roundabout – the world's first pop-up, plug-and-play theatre.

Roundabout flat packs into a lorry and pops up all over the country in theatres, school halls, warehouses, sports centres, car parks and fields.

Roundabout needs no special skills to assemble. Anyone can help put it up, the only tool you need is an Allen key. Sort of like IKEA. No piece of the auditorium takes more than two people to carry. And it's powered from 13amp plug sockets, so the whole theatre runs off the same power supply as your kettle. It uses state-of-the-art LED lighting technology to minimise energy consumption and keep us green.

'A beautifully designed masterpiece in engineering… a significant breakthrough in theatre technology.'
Winner – Theatre Building of the Year, The Stage Awards 2015

We spent four years developing Roundabout before its launch at the Edinburgh Festival in 2014. We built it because we're passionate about new plays and we want as many people as possible to be able to see them. We know that many places in the country don't have theatres. Now we can take a theatre to them.

We're proud to be present outstanding plays by some of the nation's finest writers in our Roundabout Season 2015, along with a host of fantastic guest companies and one-off performances and events.

'The @painesplough Roundabout is a beautiful, magical space.'
@evenicol on Twitter

We need your help to keep Roundabout on the road, touring the length and breadth of the UK bringing great new plays and a thrilling theatre experience to people's doorsteps. If you'd like to donate please visit our JustGiving page: **www.justgiving.com/painesplough**

www.painesplough.com/roundabout
#roundaboutpp

THE HUMAN EAR

Alexandra Wood

Thanks

Thanks to George Perrin for his invaluable, perceptive insights during the development of the play; Sian Reese-Williams and Abdul Salis for their patience, good humour and talent bringing it to life; Tom Dingle and the Jersey Arts Trust for giving me space to write; Lisa Foster and the Alan Brodie team; everyone at Paines Plough for their continued support, which means a huge amount to me.

A.W.

For Rachel and Alistair

Characters

LUCY, *twenty-six*
MAN, *late twenties*
ED

Notes on Text

MAN *and* ED *should be played by the same actor. He does not have to bear any resemblance to* LUCY.

A forward slash (/) in the text indicates a point of interruption.

Bold text should tear in and out of the scene like a piece of shrapnel passing through. This could be achieved in whatever way the director chooses but should be noticeably different from the rest of the scene.

This text went to press before the end of rehearsals and so may differ slightly from the play as performed.

ONE

The doorstep.

MAN. I wasn't sure you'd recognise me.

LUCY. Of course I recognise you Jason, of course I

MAN. Ten years.

LUCY. I was just expecting someone else, that's / all.

MAN. You might wish I was.

LUCY. What?

MAN. Someone else.

LUCY. What? No, why would I

MAN. Brother. Blood. Doesn't mean

LUCY. I can't believe you're here, it's just a shock, that's all,
just a

I'm shaking ~~I'm~~

Feel my hand ~~I'm properly~~

She offers him her hand to feel.

He doesn't.

She withdraws it.

Why didn't you call first why didn't you

~~This is~~

I don't know what to say, Jason, ~~I don't know where to~~

I'm sure you

You know about Mum.

Pause.

MAN. I had to find out from a paper.

A photo in a paper.

A photo I was in. In the original.

LUCY. I'm sorry.

MAN. The editor, the journalist, the paramedics, the police officers, the passers-by, the endless list of people who knew my mother was dead before I did.

Who told you?

LUCY. Ed.

A police officer told / me.

MAN. Came over here, did he, break it to you gently.

ED. Is there anyone you'd like me to call?

LUCY. Who?

ED. A friend, family member, partner.

MAN. Made sure you were / okay.

LUCY. There's no good way to hear it Jason, so let's not compete over

MAN. There is no competition.

LUCY. Did you come here to fight?

MAN. I shouldn't need a reason to come here.

LUCY. You don't need a / reason.

MAN. Here is my home.

You shouldn't be asking why I came here.

LUCY. I'm not.

Please.

~~I'm really~~

This hasn't started well.

You're back, I can't / believe

MAN. Not back.

LUCY. For now at least. And that's more than I've had in a long time so

MAN. Whose fault's that?

LUCY. Look at you, you're

She looks at him.

Different.

MAN. Ten years is a long time.

LUCY. You're broader, taller even.

MAN. I've always been this height.

LUCY. Well that's not true, not always, Jason, not / always.

MAN. Alright, obviously not always, but I haven't grown since I left.

LUCY. Do I look the same?

MAN. I'd know you anywhere.

LUCY. **What the fuck are you doing?**

There's too much to say so please let's not start with

That's my stuff, you're burning my fucking stuff.

MAN. Who paid for it?

LUCY. Mum! Mum paid for it you moron, how are we / supposed

MAN. And how did Mum pay for it?

LUCY. With money!

MAN. Dad's money.

LUCY. Our money!

MAN. Money he got paid to blow things up and get killed. I don't want his money, I don't want anything to do with it.

LUCY. **Every time I think you're done you find another way to make things worse.**

MAN. **This is what he died for Lucy.**

LUCY. **You can't burn everything we own, how are we supposed to live?**

MAN. ~~You can't choose where we start.~~

This duvet and those trainers and that TV and it's nothing, look at it, it's nothing.

LUCY. How you heard, ~~that's not the~~

MAN. That matters.

LUCY. It's not the *important things*

MAN. How would you feel? Finding out like that.

I hadn't seen her in ten years and there she is in the paper.

How would you feel?

Pause.

I left because of what you said.

LUCY. I never told you to leave for ever.

If you want nothing to do with it then

I never told you to

If you want nothing to do with it

I never said you couldn't call. Or visit. Or come home for good.

We didn't even know if you

If you want nothing

If you were alive.

MAN. You said you and Mum would be better off without me.

You must've known that'd kill me, if you knew me at all, and you did, better than anyone.

Better off without me.

LUCY. I didn't mean ten years, Jason, I didn't mean go and
never come back, I just / meant

MAN. You killed me.

LUCY. Don't say that.

MAN. Soon as you said it / you

LUCY. That's not fair.

MAN. Being asked to leave by my own sister isn't fair.

LUCY. You didn't exactly make it easy, did / you.

MAN. Finding out my mother's dead from a paper isn't fair.

Feeling like it's all my fault.

Is your brother in?

LUCY. Why?

MAN. Is Jason in?

LUCY. Why?

MAN. Please just answer the question miss.

LUCY. Why don't you answer mine?

MAN. We'd like to talk to him.

LUCY. Why?

MAN. Is he in?

LUCY. Do you know what happened to our dad?

MAN. I'm not aware, no.

LUCY. He was killed.

MAN. I'm sorry to hear that.

LUCY. In Kuwait.

MAN. I'm sorry to hear that miss, but

LUCY. No you're not.

**MAN. I am, but what happened to your dad is one thing,
this is another.**

LUCY. No it's not.

MAN. Is your brother in?

LUCY. Is this why you've come?

MAN. Yes. This is exactly why I've come.

LUCY. Not to see me? Not to

Doesn't it make you, what happened to Mum, doesn't it
make you want to

MAN. Forgive and forget all about it?

LUCY. We're all that's left, Jason.

ED. Is there anyone you'd like me to call?

LUCY. You're here.

I don't believe you're here to accuse me and leave.

I don't believe that.

MAN. I needed to be here before, then maybe I wouldn't have
felt like I was a curse, like it was all my fault.

LUCY. Like what was your fault?

MAN. Mum.

What happened to

LUCY. How could that possibly be your fault?

MAN. You asked me to go.

LUCY. Because of how you were being then, but

What happened to Mum was

Nothing to do with you.

MAN. Friends, other people, tried to reason with me but that
wasn't enough, I needed to hear you tell me it wasn't my
fault, that I wasn't the reason.

LUCY. There is no reason.

    Those four men might've thought they had reasons for killing innocent people but there's no reason Mum was one of them.

    None.

    Nothing you did.

    Nothing she did.

    No reason.

MAN. I needed to hear you say that.

LUCY. I'm saying it now.

MAN. But it's too late, it's too

LUCY. No it's not.

MAN. It is, it's too late it's too

LUCY. Why's it too late?

    What've you done? Why's there blood on your shirt?

MAN. It isn't blood.

LUCY. What is it then?

MAN. Paint. Red paint, that's all.

LUCY. It looks like blood, Jason, did you hurt yourself?

MAN. I'm fine.

LUCY. Let me see.

    She tries to lift up his shirt to check for a wound but he stops her.

MAN. I'm fine Lucy.

LUCY. Did you hurt someone else then?

    Jason.

MAN. It's paint, that's all.

LUCY. It's not too late Jason.

Come inside.

MAN *shakes his head*.

Please. It's your home.

MAN *shakes his head*.

It probably looks the same.

We redecorated a few years ago, just to freshen the place up, nothing major, just some / paint.

MAN. I don't care.

I don't care about the colour of the walls and the curtains, I didn't come here to hear about that, I didn't come here to

LUCY. You don't have to stay long if you don't want.

MAN. You're expecting someone.

LUCY. That doesn't matter.

MAN. I didn't come here to

I don't want to sit around sipping tea and

LUCY. Beer then?

MAN. I didn't come here / to

LUCY. You can alter your plans can't you?

MAN. You killed me Lucy.

A cup of tea's not / going

LUCY. I don't like you knocking. I don't like answering the door, not knowing who it is.

ED. Okay, well, perhaps I could do a special knock.

LUCY. I can't stand the sound of it Ed, it's the sound I can't

ED. Alright, I could call you instead. How about that?

When I'm outside the house, I'll call, and you can answer the door, knowing it's me.

LUCY. Or I could just give you this.

She offers him a key.

ED. We've only been together a few weeks, Lucy, isn't it a bit soon / to be

LUCY. It's just easier, I prefer it.

ED. Are you sure, because it

LUCY. **I said so didn't I?**

   No need to knock.

   Just take it will you.

   ED *takes the key.*

   Where do you live?

   Pause.

   Don't worry, I'm not going to hunt you down.

MAN. Never did before.

LUCY. I tried, but it's not easy to find someone who doesn't want to be found.

MAN. Scotland.

LUCY. Scotland?

   Edinburgh or

MAN. That's not the only place in Scotland.

LUCY. I know that.

   There's Glasgow too.

MAN. Inverness.

LUCY. That's north, isn't it, that's

MAN. We were just outside.

LUCY. We?

   Are you married or

   Pause.

I'm not.

I'm with someone. It's new but

That's who I thought you were. Ed.

He's a copper.

MAN. I shouldn't try anything then.

LUCY. Try anything?

MAN. You a copper too?

LUCY. Nurse.

I'm on leave at the moment, but

Unpaid.

I did go back but I spat at a patient so they thought I should take more time.

She suggested I get a dog. The old lady. She'd heard about Mum and she suggested I get a dog. Like a replacement or something. She's lucky I only spat. There was a scalpel there and I very nearly

MAN. what happened to your dad is one thing, this is another.

LUCY. No it's not.

MAN. Is your brother in?

LUCY. I could've done something, in that moment.

Pause.

MAN. It said Mum was a legal secretary. How long had she been doing that?

LUCY. Eight years.

MAN. So she rebuilt a life, managed to find a new

That's what I wanted. I didn't stay away out of spite or because I'd forgotten or didn't care, it's very important you understand that.

LUCY. Why?

MAN. I need you to know that.

   You had each other. That's all that comforted me.

LUCY. Not now.

ED. Is there anyone you'd like me to call?

LUCY. What do you do in Inverness?

ED. Is there anyone / you'd

LUCY. Are you a history teacher?

MAN. A history teacher?

LUCY. You were set on that. For a while.

MAN. A history teacher?

LUCY. You don't remember? Mr Duval. You basically wanted to be him.

MAN. No, I

LUCY. Seriously?

   He was an expert on the French Revolution. You went on and on about it.

MAN. The French Revolution?

LUCY. Liberté! Égalité! Fraternité! Every breakfast. You seriously don't

   Maybe you just liked his accent. I swear you actually started to sound French.

MAN. Need a degree to teach.

LUCY. Yeah, well you planned to go to uni.

MAN. Never even

LUCY. I mean, plans change so

MAN. I'm a carpenter so

LUCY. A carpenter?

MAN. Furniture-maker really, nothing to do with

LUCY. Where did that come from?

MAN. I don't know.

I enjoy it.

LUCY. And you make a living?

MAN. I'm not bad. I'm actually quite good.

LUCY. I didn't mean that, it just sounds like one of those jobs where it might be difficult to make a living.

MAN. Never relied on anyone else to support me.

LUCY. That's not what I meant Jason.

It's just a bit of a surprise, not like any of us were particularly handy.

MAN. A good chair can

A good chair can

A good chair

He puts his hand in his pocket.

Pause.

LUCY. I've been wanting a built-in wardrobe for ages, are you any good at those?

MAN. I haven't even stepped in the house yet and you're / already

LUCY. I'm joking, of course I'm

Yet?

So you will come in eventually?

I promise not to put you to work.

Not immediately, / anyway.

MAN. A history teacher?

LUCY. Interests change.

> And a carpenter's far more useful so I'm not / complaining

MAN. A good chair, like a Sam Maloof chair, can make your day better.

LUCY. He your guru?

> *He takes a Sam Maloof dollhouse chair out of his pocket.*
>
> *He shows her.*
>
> Is that for a dollhouse?
>
> MAN *smiles.*

MAN. I thought I was buying a full-size one. I'd never bought anything online before, I went on to everyone about how I got a really great price and then

> Then this arrived.
>
> LUCY *laughs.*
>
> One of my
>
> Someone made a model of me, a mini me, to sit in it. So it didn't go to waste.

LUCY. You always carry it on you?

MAN. You can't tell much from a model but he's a master.

LUCY. I like it.

> *She goes to take it but he holds on to it.*
>
> Can I see it?

MAN. Not much to see.

> *He puts it back in his pocket.*
>
> *Pause.*
>
> I don't know what I'm doing here.

LUCY. This is exactly where you should be.

ED. Is there anyone you'd like me to call?

LUCY. I'm sorry for what I said.

    If you came here for an apology I'll happily give you one.

    I never meant you to leave without a word, and I think you should've been in touch, but you're right, I do know you, and I knew what I said would hurt you and I'm sorry. This is where you should be. I'm better off with you here.

ED. Is there anyone / you'd

LUCY. We're connected in a unique way.

ED. Is there any/one

LUCY. There will be no more brothers or sisters ever again.

    We're it.

ED. Any/one

LUCY. Our parents are dead but we're not alone. Or we don't have to be at least.

    A knock at the door.

MAN. You don't know me.

LUCY. Don't you want to find the good in what's happened?

MAN. Good?

    No good can come from this.

LUCY. It can.

    If it brings us back together, that's something.

    You shouldn't be knocking at the door, like a stranger.

    She goes inside for a moment.

    She returns and offers him a key.

    Take it, Jason, it's yours.

MAN. I can't take that.

LUCY. It's yours.

You shouldn't have to knock. This is your home too.

Please. I want you to have it.

He takes the key.

TWO

The hallway.

LUCY. Why are you knocking? Don't knock, I told you, that's why I gave you a key.

ED. I'm on duty, so

LUCY. I thought you'd be here earlier.

ED. Something's happened / which

LUCY. It's a shame you weren't, you could've met someone.

ED. I didn't want to use the key because I'm here in an official capacity, Lucy, and it's not appropriate.

LUCY. Never been too bothered about appropriate in the past.

ED. Well I am bothered / I am

LUCY. Which is good, who wants appropriate.

ED. I come in the door with a key, that suggests we're

LUCY. That we know each other, Ed, that's all, that I trust you not to steal my stuff, / that I

ED. I'm here as an officer, I'm

Shall we go into the sitting room?

LUCY. Somewhere more comfortable?

ED. I'm serious, Lucy, I'm trying to be

LUCY. Alright, I can see that.

But guess who was here.

Just knocked on the door, out of the blue, no warning, / no

MAN. We could be living in the third century.

LUCY. How?

MAN. When Robespierre proclaimed France a republic in seventeen ninety-two they turned the clock back to zero.

LUCY. We're not in France.

MAN. They just started again. Invented a whole new calendar so the church meant nothing, everything that had gone before meant nothing.

LUCY. Is Mr Duval even French?

MAN. What's that got to do with it?

LUCY. Can you pass the honey.

MAN. Imagine the ambition of that. Wiping away the whole of Christianity, your king, and just saying, no, we're starting again, we're starting from now.

ED. This isn't easy, Lucy, what I've got to say so can we please just focus / on

LUCY. Can't you see I'm happy, Ed? More than

Can't you let me enjoy this moment a little bit before we talk about the investigation?

ED. I'm not here to talk about your mum.

LUCY. Fine, whatever it is, can you just let me enjoy the feeling of having my brother back before / bringing

ED. What?

LUCY. Jason was here.

Literally a few hours ago, he just knocked on the / door

ED. What are you talking about?

LUCY. Just standing there on the doorstep / without a

ED. No, Lucy.

LUCY. He was.

ED. No, Lucy, no, there's no way / he

LUCY. He was, Ed, right here. We talked. He didn't want to come in, but we talked and it / was

ED. They found his body, Lucy.

LUCY. What?

Pause.

ED. That's why I'm here, that's

To tell you he's

LUCY. **I'm shaking I'm**

He was just here.

Feel my hand I'm properly

ED. He's dead, Lucy.

LUCY. Obviously there's been a mistake, I'm not crazy, he was right here.

ED. It's not a mistake.

I'm so sorry.

LUCY. But he only left a couple of hours ago, he was

Of course I

ED. He died five days ago, at least.

LUCY. What are you talking about I don't understand a word you're saying it doesn't make sense he was right here on this doorstep.

Of course I

Ask a neighbour. Someone will have seen him he wasn't a figment of my, I wasn't standing here talking to myself / for

ED. Jason died five days ago.

>**ED** *kisses her.*
>
>**I'm so sorry, I shouldn't have done that. That was unforgivable, completely, I don't know what came over me, I've never done anything like that before, / I**

LUCY. You've got it wrong.

ED. They found his body in Scotland.

LUCY. Scotland?

MAN. That's not the only place in Scotland.

ED. Just outside Inverness.

LUCY. **That's north, isn't it, that's**

>No, that doesn't
>
>That's where he was living but that / doesn't

ED. And that's where he died.

LUCY. **She's dead, isn't she?**

>No.

ED. In a forest, in the Highlands.

LUCY. She was on that bus, wasn't she?

ED. I'm very sorry.

>*Silence.*
>
>**Is there anyone you'd like me to call?**

LUCY. Who?

ED. Come here, Luce, let me

>*He tries to hug her but she backs away.*

LUCY. I don't need a hug 'cause it isn't him.

ED. A forestry worker found an ear, it was a miracle he even noticed / it

LUCY. Just an ear?

ED. The body wasn't in one piece.

   It's a wilderness up there, Lucy, wild animals must've

LUCY. What? Torn it to pieces?

ED. No, just

LUCY. If that's the case how can they possibly know it's him?

ED. They've got records from his time at Feltham, he's on the system.

LUCY. What would Jason be doing in a forest?

ED. He probably wanted to be away from

   To be alone.

   Because he

   He killed himself.

LUCY. Why would he

MAN. But it's too late, it's too

LUCY. No it's not.

MAN. It is, it's too late it's too

LUCY. Why's it too late?

ED. I don't know who knocked on your door Lucy.

MAN. Someone else.

LUCY. Sorry?

ED. He may have looked like Jason, he may have known details about Jason's life, but I can assure / you

LUCY. There'll be an explanation. Things sometimes look one way when they are in / fact

ED. He shot himself.

LUCY. Jason didn't have a gun.

ED. You hadn't seen him in years.

LUCY. Where d'you get a gun, I don't know where you, do normal people know where to get guns?

ED. Your brother wasn't completely

LUCY. Why are you speaking like that?

MAN (*in a French accent*). Like what?

LUCY. What do you know about my brother?

ED. That he's dead.

That he shot himself in the Highlands at least five days ago.

So it can't be him who knocked at the door.

Pause.

LUCY. I don't know what to

MAN. Someone else.

LUCY. What am I supposed to

MAN. Came over here, did he, break it to you / gently.

LUCY. I don't understand.

ED. No.

LUCY. No I really, I might be going crazy Ed.

ED. You're not.

A knock at the door.

LUCY. He looked like him, he could've

MAN. I'd know you anywhere.

LUCY. How could he know

ED. It's perfectly natural, Lucy, to think we see people we love, people we've lost, when it's not

MAN. A history teacher?

LUCY. We spoke, Ed, we had a

MAN. A history / teacher?

LUCY. a whole conversation, maybe I am mad.

ED. You're not.

LUCY. But I felt something. Didn't even question it.

I felt like I had my brother back, and yes he was a bit angry at first / but

ED. Did he threaten you?

LUCY. He had his reasons, he wasn't looking to

He had a dollhouse chair for God's sake, / he wasn't

ED. A chair?

LUCY. A dollhouse chair. He bought it online, thought he was buying a full-size one, went on about it to everyone, which sounds like Jason, / and then this dollhouse chair arrives, this Sam Maloof, he's a furniture-maker, his guru

MAN. They just started again. Invented a whole new calendar so the church meant nothing, everything that had gone before meant nothing.

LUCY. I had my brother back. For two hours I've been thinking I'm not alone any more, the world was better because I had my brother back so please don't tell me it wasn't real Ed.

ED. I'm here.

You're not alone.

LUCY. **I'm shaking I'm**

Feel my hand I'm properly

You haven't seen the body, it wasn't even in one piece, it's possible, isn't it possible it's not him.

ED *shakes his head*.

What kind of sister would mistake someone else, someone

ED. It's natural, Luce, when you've / lost

LUCY. Don't say that, don't say it's

ED. But it is. What you've been through, it's only natural you'll

LUCY. I gave him a key.

ED. What?

LUCY. I gave him a key Ed.

ED. To the house?

LUCY *nods*.

Why did you

LUCY. It's Jason's house too.

ED. But that isn't Jason, that's

She's an old lady, Lucy, she didn't mean to upset you.

LUCY. She's lucky that's all I did.

There was a scalpel right there.

ED. A scalpel?

LUCY. There's no need to look at me like that.

ED. Well what d'you mean?

LUCY. She's lucky I didn't cut out her tongue that's what I mean, she's lucky I didn't

Stop looking at me like that.

ED. Okay, that's okay, we can change the locks, it's fine.

LUCY. But how will he feel, if it is Jason, how will he feel if he can't get in?

ED. We don't know who he is Lucy.

MAN. If you knew me at all

LUCY. I did know him, Ed, better than anyone.

ED. I'm sure you did, but

> The ear, that was one of the things they used to identify him, they're unique, like fingerprints. No one else on this planet has that ear. It's his body. I'm sorry Lucy, but it is.

> Con artists are ruthless, they have / no

LUCY. Kiss me again.

ED. **Are you sure? Are you**

> They prey on people when they're vulnerable,

> **I don't know what came over me Lucy, I've never**

> when they're looking for comfort, reasons, / which is

LUCY. Like when you kissed me.

ED. What? That's not the same at all.

LUCY. From the outside it could look the same, it / could

ED. I'd never take advantage of

LUCY. I know that Ed.

ED. I'm a professional, not a

> It's my job to look after you and I / don't

LUCY. Your job?

ED. As your

LUCY. Family Liaison Officer.

ED. No, as your, well yes, but

LUCY. He's my family.

ED. As someone who cares about you.

LUCY. When you kissed me you said it was against the rules, entirely the wrong moment, but something overwhelming had compelled you.

> ED *nods*.

Well something overwhelming tells me this is Jason.

Does that mean nothing?

ED. It means you miss him.

LUCY. What about instinct? Gut. That's how we survive. If I can't even trust that how the hell am I going to survive?

How am I going to

Pause.

ED. We could go to Inverness. To see his body, it might help you to

LUCY. Of course I

ED. Speak to some of his friends maybe.

LUCY. Of course I

ED. See where he lived, worked.

LUCY. Of course I

ED. It might help.

LUCY. I gave him a key Ed.

ED. That's okay, don't worry, we'll change the locks.

And I'll be here as much as I can.

You're not alone Lucy, okay?

THREE

The landing.

LUCY. Jason?

    If someone's here just say something.

    There's nothing to take.

    Just say something and you can have whatever you want, just say something I hate the quiet, I can't stand the

    Please just / say something please just

    MAN *enters*.

MAN. It's me, Lucy, it's me.

    I'm sorry, / I didn't mean to

LUCY. What are you doing here?

MAN. I didn't mean to scare you.

LUCY. You didn't scare me you / just

MAN. I should've let you know I was coming round.

    I just wanted to see my room.

LUCY. So you just let yourself in / you just

MAN. Sorry, it's

    You did give me a key so I thought / it'd be

LUCY. So you just let yourself in just

MAN. I thought it'd be alright but I should've knocked.

LUCY. Don't knock, don't

    You can't / just

MAN. I'm sorry, Luce. You gave me a key and I just thought

    A knock at the door.

LUCY. I know I did, I did give you a key so

ED. A forestry worker found an ear

LUCY. Did you find what you were looking for?

MAN. I wasn't looking for anything, just

LUCY. Is it the same as you remember?

MAN. Let's go downstairs, have a cup of tea or something.

LUCY. Now you want tea.

MAN. I scared you, I'm sorry / let's just

LUCY. I'm fine.

   Pause.

   Is it as you imagined?

MAN. Imagined?

   I guessed you'd probably use it as a study or something, and
   you do so

LUCY. Wasn't much of a bedroom after you burnt all your stuff.

   Pause.

MAN. I was thinking about the French Revolution last night
   and the thing is, I don't remember very much about it.

LUCY. Well you know what they say.

MAN. No.

LUCY. If you remember it you weren't really there.

MAN. As you said, maybe I was just affected by the teacher's
   passion for it.

LUCY. Mr Duval.

MAN. Mr Duval. When someone's passionate about something
   it's infectious, isn't it, so maybe I was just swept up / in

LUCY. Wasn't just the French Revolution. You always liked
   history, even before Mr Duval.

MAN. I guess I just

> Interests change, don't they, evolve.

LUCY. You were never into carpentry before so yeah, obviously interests change.

> It doesn't matter Jason.

> **Do you want some fish?**

> I'm not going to quiz you on the key events of the French Revolution. There's no test.

ED. No, I'm

LUCY. I made her dinner.

> **It needed to be used so I made her dinner.**

> **But I knew she'd never eat it. As I was making it I knew she'd never eat it.**

> **Do you want some?**

ED. No, I'm fine, thank you.

LUCY. Must be hungry.

> **Must be tired. Do you want to sit down?**

ED. How about you Lucy? Can I call you Lucy?

LUCY. Of course you can, that's my name.

ED. Let's sit down.

LUCY. I don't want to.

ED. Okay.

LUCY. Moment you sit back and

> **That's when they strike, moment you**

ED. No one's going to

LUCY. Was she sitting? Did she have a seat?

ED. I don't know Lucy.

LUCY. They didn't know anything about her.

ED. No.

LUCY. **They didn't know anything about her.**

   ED *shakes his head.*

   Have I changed?

MAN. I'd know you anywhere.

LUCY. It's been a long time, is there nothing different about me?

   He looks at her.

   It's not a trick question.

MAN. You're more sophisticated. Not wearing that Kickers
   T-shirt at least.

LUCY. That was the height of fashion.

MAN. At the time maybe.

   In your group maybe.

   It never was.

LUCY. It was.

ED. Is there anyone you'd like me / to

LUCY. You'll remember things I don't. About me. Us.

MAN. I don't know if I

LUCY. Anything.

MAN. I was always thinking about you.

LUCY. Thinking what?

MAN. Missing you, I don't know, just missing

LUCY. What?

MAN. We haven't spent enough time together for me to know if
   you've

LUCY. Do you want to know about me?

MAN. Of course I do.

LUCY. **Of course I**

So ask me things.

You haven't asked.

MAN. You'll tell me what you want, I don't want to force you.

LUCY. Don't you want to know about my friends and whether I still swim five times a week and how I've been / and

MAN. I can imagine how you've been.

LUCY. You don't have to imagine, I'm here, just ask me.

MAN. I don't want to interrogate you, / I don't

LUCY. I was only out for an hour.

Did you wait for me to leave before you came in?

MAN. Of course I didn't.

LUCY. **Of course I**

Don't sneak in and just stand / here

MAN. I didn't sneak in, you gave me a key.

LUCY. Don't stand in an empty room looking for answers, what's that going to tell you?

ED. Is there anyone you'd like me to / call?

LUCY. Why come back if it's not for me?

There's no one else here, so I don't know what you

A knock at the door.

Ask me.

MAN. I don't know where to

Knocking at the door.

LUCY. Ask about my swimming.

MAN. Do you still swim five times a week?

LUCY. Train. When you do something that much it's training.

MAN. Do you?

LUCY. No.

MAN. Okay.

More knocking.

LUCY. Ask me why then.

MAN. This is

LUCY. Ask me.

MAN. It feels unnatural Lucy, it feels

Pause.

Why not?

LUCY. At sixteen, seventeen, I had to decide whether to go for it or not. I decided against it.

MAN. it's too late

LUCY. Go on.

MAN. Why?

LUCY. I wanted to but Mum needed me.

She wasn't good when you left, I couldn't be at the pool day and night.

So I stopped.

Pause.

How am I going to

MAN. That must've been hard.

LUCY. It was.

MAN. You'd done it for years.

LUCY. I had.

MAN. All those early mornings.

LUCY. What would you know about those?

LUCY *smiles*.

MAN. Never been a morning person.

I was jealous though.

LUCY. No you weren't.

MAN. I was.

LUCY. Not at five in the morning you weren't.

MAN. When you were training, you didn't have the strength to think about anything else and it was bliss, you said.

LUCY. Did I?

MAN. I remember 'cause I was jealous.

Maybe if I'd had something like that I would've

Pause.

LUCY. Mark's done very well.

MAN. Mark?

LUCY. You remember / Mark.

MAN. Oh I remember Mark.

LUCY. So. Ask me if he still swims.

MAN. It isn't a conversation if you tell me what to say.

LUCY. So initiate something.

MAN. might wish I was.

LUCY. What?

MAN. Does Mark still swim?

LUCY. Yes.

MAN. might wish I / was.

LUCY. Aiming for Beijing.

MAN. Beijing?

LUCY. The Olympics.

MAN. Yeah I know, that's

Well he was always very

Talented.

LUCY. You always seemed to think so.

MAN. Are you still in touch?

LUCY. Why? D'you want his number?

MAN. No thanks.

LUCY. He's pretty busy with training and travel but

MAN. He was always a bit of a

LUCY. What?

MAN. You know how he is.

LUCY. How is he?

MAN. A bit of a prick.

LUCY *laughs*.

LUCY. You were happy enough to watch him swim.

MAN. He used to do that thing, slapping himself on the chest before the race started.

He demonstrates.

Look at me, I'm such a man.

LUCY. Just hyping himself up.

MAN. No one else felt the need.

LUCY. No one else won as much as he did / so

MAN. He looked ridiculous.

LUCY. He's my friend.

MAN. Has he even called since Mum died?

LUCY. Own brother didn't call so

MAN. Here now.

ED. No one else on this planet has

MAN. That's completely different.

> *Pause.*

> Glad to hear he's doing well, anyway.

LUCY. I told Ed about you.

MAN. The copper?

> LUCY *nods.*

> Okay.

LUCY. Is it?

MAN. Yeah, I mean

> I'm not sure I'm ready to start meeting people yet, I only came to

LUCY. Sit in an empty room?

ED. it's only natural / you'll

LUCY. He's never met you before.

MAN. I know that.

LUCY. So I would've thought that's easier than seeing someone like Mark. Never met so

MAN. It's not my place to vet him or anything, Luce.

LUCY. I'm not asking you to.

> He was more interested in vetting you.

MAN. Why?

LUCY. He's worried.

> **Why are you speaking like that?**

MAN (*in a French accent*). Like what?

> Why's he

LUCY. Can't be Jason, he said.

MAN. Why's that?

    Never even met me, as you say.

LUCY. Do you hunt?

MAN. Do / I

LUCY. They do that up there, don't they? In Scotland.

MAN. What makes him think it can't be me?

LUCY. Do you hunt?

MAN. What's that got to do with / anything?

LUCY. Do you?

MAN. No, Lucy, I don't hunt.

LUCY. What is it then?

MAN. Paint. Red paint, that's all.

LUCY. I'm just asking.

MAN. Did I ever express any interest in shooting at / things?

LUCY. Interests change, don't they? Evolve.

    It's an outdoor pursuit, and it's a wilderness up / there.

MAN. There are plenty of things to do that don't involve / shooting at

LUCY. So you don't have a gun?

MAN. No, why would I

    There are plenty / of things

LUCY. It's a wilderness.

MAN. Some of it, so there are other things / that

LUCY. Like what?

MAN. Like, I don't know, like normal things. Walking, swimming, open-water swimming, in lochs and rivers and / firths

LUCY. So why are you here?

MAN. You shouldn't be asking why I / came here.

LUCY. If there's so much up there, why are you here?

MAN. You.

LUCY. Don't just say you

MAN. You killed / me.

LUCY. Don't just say that because you think that's / what I

MAN. I'm not.

LUCY. I killed you, you don't / want

MAN. I shouldn't have said / that.

LUCY. What you believe, isn't it?

Pause.

You don't want anything to do with me. So why are you still here? Why are you in the house?

She takes his hand. He flinches.

MAN. What are you doing?

She feels the palm of his hand.

LUCY. Rough hands.

MAN. Thanks.

LUCY. Been doing manual work.

MAN. Told you I have.

LUCY. You seem real.

MAN. Is your brother in?

LUCY. Did something happen?

To make you come back.

MAN. Mum.

LUCY. It's been three months.

MAN. I needed time to

LUCY. To?

Pause.

MAN. Have you ever been wild swimming? I think you'd like / it.

LUCY. To what?

MAN. You wanted me to ask you things Lucy, so tell me.

LUCY. Is that what you've been doing the last three months? Swimming outside in the cold?

MAN. Someone has to pay.

LUCY. Why?

MAN. Because they

LUCY. Are you caught up in something?

MAN. Like what?

LUCY. I don't know.

MAN. **That can't just be it, Lucy, that can't just be the end**

Caught up in something? I'm not a

LUCY. I'm just trying to work out why you're here all of a sudden.

MAN. Caught up in something?

LUCY. There's no need to act all indignant, there's a reason / I'm asking.

MAN. I was sixteen.

LUCY. It's a valid question, isn't it?

MAN. No, it's not, this is exactly why I was afraid to come back.

LUCY. But you have, you have come back.

MAN. Caught up in something, is that who you think I am?

LUCY. I don't know, how am I supposed to / know

MAN. that can't just be the end, as if he never mattered

LUCY. I haven't seen you.

MAN. You're seeing me now.

LUCY. You're different.

MAN. Of course I'm different, / it's

LUCY. So how am I supposed to know?

MAN. I'm not a bigot, you know that, and obviously a pig's head can't fix anything, I wish I'd never done it and I'll never forgive myself now, but you sent / me away

LUCY. Now?

What d'you mean never will now?

MAN. What d'you think I mean?

LUCY. You're dead.

I killed you.

MAN. Someone has to pay.

LUCY. Why?

MAN. Because they have to.

Why aren't you

He's dead, how can you

They killed him, / how

LUCY. He was a soldier, Jason, he knew the / risks

MAN. We'll never see Dad again, and you expect me / to

LUCY. You can't change that.

MAN. Why don't you care?

LUCY. You really think I don't care?

MAN. That can't just be it, Lucy, that can't just be the end, as if he never mattered, that can't just / be

LUCY. So take revenge.

MAN. it's too late, it's / too

LUCY. Do something to make yourself feel better.

MAN. it's too late it's too

LUCY. That's why you're here isn't / it?

MAN. if you knew me at all

LUCY. That's why you've come.

MAN. and you did.

LUCY. So go on.

MAN. I don't know what you / mean.

LUCY. Yes you do, you can think of something, take revenge.

MAN. You think I want to hurt you?

LUCY. I killed you, so go on.

MAN. I shouldn't have said / that.

LUCY. I sent you away.

   Failed you.

   Killed you, even.

MAN. I shouldn't have said / that.

LUCY. But you did, you did say it, so this is your chance.

MAN. You gave me a key. Why give me a key if you think I'm
   here to hurt you?

LUCY. Key, no key, that's not going to save me is it?

MAN. We could be living in the / third

LUCY. Exactly, the third century, changing the locks won't save
   me now. If someone / wants

ED. A scalpel?

LUCY. **There's no need to look at me like that.** If someone
wants to hurt you they'll find a way, don't need a scalpel,
don't even need a dog, just the word dog is enough, just the

So go on.

Silence.

MAN *shakes his head.*

MAN. I just want you to tell me about the French Revolution.

I can't remember anything about it.

LUCY. Neither can I, you were the one / who

MAN. I'm scared I'll lose

I won't remember.

Pause.

LUCY. They had a new calendar, I remember that.

Turned the clock back to zero.

We could be living in the third century, I remember that.

FOUR

The hallway.

ED. There's no point me standing here telling you he can't be Jason, that he's lying to you, that he could be dangerous, that's not going to convince you because it's just words, and you felt something and words can't compete with that so

LUCY. Why are you talking like that?

ED. Like what?

Like what, Lucy?

LUCY. Sorry, I

ED. I went to Inverness.

For proof. Physical, undeniable proof that Jason is dead and this man is lying.

And it's no good me standing here telling you I've seen his body, it's just more words, so I brought you evidence.

Knocking at the door.

LUCY. What evidence?

ED. Ears are unique.

I've got his ear, the one that was

LUCY. Jason's?

ED *presents her with a transparent plastic freezer bag. Inside is a human ear.*

She stares at it.

That's my brother's ear?

The sound of a bonfire working its way through a family's possessions.

You stole my brother's ear?

ED. I didn't steal it, you're his sister, it's

LUCY. If you want nothing to do with it / then

ED. I mean, okay, yes, I shouldn't have taken it but

LUCY. Then why don't you go Jason?

ED. It's important that you see.

LUCY. Just go.

LUCY *takes the bag and looks more closely at the ear.*

ED. It's his, Lucy.

She takes it out of the plastic bag and holds it in the palm of her hand.

I risked my job to

LUCY. Could be anyone's.

ED. It's Jason's.

LUCY. You don't have to keep saying it.

You think I'd feel something, some recognition, something.

But I don't.

Can you smell that?

ED. I don't think it smells Lucy, I've kept it / cold.

LUCY. Not flesh, not

Smoke.

ED. Smoke? No. Look I know it's a slightly extreme action to take, but it's proof, Lucy.

ED *takes out a photograph of Jason, a side profile, from his time at Feltham.*

LUCY. What's that?

ED. It's so you can compare them.

She takes the photo and looks at it closely.

They're identical, look.

The sound of a teenage swimmer beating his bare chest to pump himself up before a race.

The shape of the helix, that's the outer-rim bit here, the lobe, the antitragus just above it, the concha, that's this bit, the antihelical fold, the fossa in there. Identical.

It's science, Lucy.

LUCY. Just to prove my brother's dead?

ED. So you know you can't trust this man, he's a liar.

I know it's extreme, it's not something I'd normally do, but I don't know how to help.

The sound of spray paint being used to write big letters on a wall.

I went up there to see for myself. You were so convinced you'd seen Jason, and I thought, well maybe she has. Maybe it isn't his body. Maybe we have got it wrong. So I went up there to find out for myself, satisfy my doubts, your doubts.

LUCY. Of course / I

ED. When I saw it really was him, that there was no mistake, I just took the ear, it was one of those impulsive decisions, like kissing you, like

LUCY. This is nothing like kissing me.

ED. No, okay, but it felt like the right thing, so I did it.

And I hope you can see that my intentions are good.

The sound of the bonfire.

I pulled a sickie, took Friday off, got the train up there. I've never considered pulling a sickie before, not for anyone, let alone getting into a morgue under false pretences, let alone taking an actual human body part, these are things I never would've done, before, but when it comes to you I seem to be more reckless.

LUCY. What am I supposed to do with it?

ED. I can deal with it for you.

LUCY. Deal with it?

ED. Return it, or

LUCY. Or

ED. I can take care of it.

LUCY. What, feed and water it regularly?

ED. I didn't mean it to upset you Lucy.

She puts the ear back in the bag.

I'd kill for you.

LUCY. What?

MAN. You killed me.

LUCY. Don't say that.

ED. Mum used to say she'd kill for me and Ben, it always made me feel safe.

I want you to feel safe, I want / you

LUCY. That's not in your control.

ED. I'll do what I can though, that's / all I

LUCY. You can't prove it, so what's it mean?

You're the one obsessed with proof.

You're the one who brought an ear from Inverness just to prove my brother's dead.

ED. And that the man at the door, the man you gave a key to, isn't Jason.

LUCY. I don't care.

The sound of spray paint being used to leave an angry message.

I'm not getting the locks changed.

ED. He isn't Jason, that's a fact.

LUCY. Okay.

ED. He's lying to you.

LUCY. It's not as simple as that.

ED. It is, Lucy, it absolutely is.

  He could be involved in Jason's death for all you know.

LUCY. He killed himself.

ED. We don't know that for sure, they're still investigating.

LUCY. So why are you stealing evidence?

ED. To prove, Lucy, to show / you

LUCY. You make out things are simple when they're not Ed.

ED. You don't know who this man is. That's simple enough
   isn't it? You don't know what he wants, why he's here, why
   he's claiming to be Jason. Correct me if I'm wrong.

LUCY. I think he knew Jason.

ED. That explains how he knows certain things, but why's he
   lying to you?

  It's strange behaviour, Lucy, at best.

LUCY. Like bringing someone a chewed-off ear?

ED. That's not the same, you can see what I was / trying to

LUCY. Why not?

ED. Because you can see I was trying to help.

LUCY. It could look very strange, Ed, can't you see that?

ED. You don't know what kind of world your brother was
   mixed up in, what kind of people he / knew.

LUCY. He was a carpenter.

ED. You can't deny his history, you can't deny he'd done
   things. He spent a year at Feltham, who'd he meet there? So
   even if he did know Jason, this man, that doesn't put my
   mind at rest, to be honest.

LUCY. I'm not changing the locks.

ED. You have to.

Knocking at the door.

LUCY. If someone wants to hurt you, they'll find a way.

ED. What kind of attitude's that?

LUCY. It's true.

I should know, don't you think.

ED. But there are things you can do to protect yourself.

LUCY. No there aren't, not really.

ED. It doesn't mean you should be reckless.

LUCY. You were, you just said.

ED. Not with your safety.

LUCY. Pulled a sickie, lied your way into a morgue, risked your job, that's reckless.

ED. It's different.

LUCY. Why? Because it's you?

We share something, Ed. I can't explain it any more than that, and I shouldn't have to.

ED. I'll have to report it, Lucy.

LUCY. Report what?

How am I going / to

ED. Him. It's suspicious behaviour. I can't ignore it. I can't let you abandon all caution, just because you feel something.

I'll do what I have to to protect you.

LUCY. You don't have to do this.

ED. If he's innocent, / if it's all just a misunderstanding, he'll have // nothing to worry about.

LUCY. / If I can't even trust

// How the hell am I

ED *kisses her.*

ED. I'm so sorry, that was unforgivable, I don't know what came over me, I've never / done anything

LUCY. You act like **How** everything's clear-cut, Ed, when it's **How** not. You kissed me when **How am I** you shouldn't have, you stole evidence, **How am I How am I** you're not spotless, and that's **if I can't even** okay, because no one is, but you seem / to think

ED. Nothing I've done's put you in danger.

LUCY. Could say you preyed on me.

ED. Is that what you believe?

LUCY. You're not innocent Ed,

How the hell am I going to

none of us / are.

ED. At least I'm honest.

You don't know who he is. Whatever you feel for him, he's not been honest, Lucy. You can't deny that.

LUCY. If you report him **How How** that's the end.

ED. You don't know him.

LUCY. I do.

ED. What's his name?

Pause.

Where's he from?

Pause.

Why's he here?

He has a key to your home.

LUCY. So do you.

ED *offers her his key.*

I don't **How am I** want it back, Ed.

ED. Take it.

For now, at least.

LUCY. That's not what I'm **How am I going to** saying, I don't want it back, keep it. **How am I going / to**

ED. I thought the ear would be enough but obviously it's not, and I need you to see I'm serious, so don't make me ask again, Luce, / take the key.

LUCY. How am I going to

She takes it back.

FIVE

The kitchen.

LUCY. Do you want a drink?

MAN. You don't have to wait on me.

ED. The shape of the / helix

LUCY. I won't be, don't worry. But it's a pretty standard thing to offer someone when they come to your house.

MAN. Our house.

ED. The / lobe

LUCY. Yeah, our

I don't want you feeling like a guest.

ED. The anti/tragus

LUCY. You're not a guest you're

> Make your own tea then.

MAN. Do you want one?

LUCY. Except you don't really know where anything is so

MAN. I think I can probably work it out.

> That's the kettle, right?

> That's the fridge.

> That's the **antitragus.**

LUCY. What?

MAN. Where you get water from.

LUCY. Right.

MAN. So I think I've got it.

> Do you want a tea?

ED. like finger/prints

LUCY. You don't have to wait / on me.

MAN. Do you want one Lucy?

LUCY. You can have a beer or something if you'd prefer.

MAN. It's ten in the morning.

LUCY. I wouldn't judge.

MAN. I don't drink, anyway.

LUCY. You don't drink?

ED. the antihelical fold

LUCY. Right.

MAN. People always react that way.

LUCY. What way?

MAN. I haven't got a **helix**, I just don't like the taste, it's a valid reason.

LUCY. Like to stay on your toes.

MAN. **Fossa?**

LUCY. Alert at all times.

MAN. Just doesn't do anything for me.

So was that yes to tea?

LUCY *nods*.

Great.

He looks at the various cupboards.

Teabags?

No, don't tell me.

He looks at the cupboards.

Have you changed things round **the fossa?**

LUCY. Maybe, I can't remember.

MAN. I probably didn't make much tea before, probably never knew where **the concha** was.

LUCY. Don't worry about it, I'm not really thirsty.

MAN. No, you wanted one, I can **lobe** it.

LUCY. It doesn't matter.

MAN. Where are **the helix**?

LUCY. It doesn't matter, really it doesn't.

Pause.

You don't have an accent.

ED. the antihelical / fold

LUCY. A Scottish accent.

MAN. Don't pick them up that quickly, do you?

LUCY. Mark sounded American after a summer's training camp.

MAN. Yeah but **lobe**'s a

LUCY. What?

MAN. I shouldn't be rude about Mark.

LUCY. Why not?

MAN. He's your friend, it's not

LUCY. Don't want to / offend me?

ED. the concha, the fossa, the antihelical fold

LUCY. Never held back before.

MAN. Alright, well Mark's a **helix** twat who probably thought
  he'd get more women by putting on a **concha** accent. Bet
  you anything he turned up the English accent when he was
  antitragus.

LUCY. We're all capable of shape-shifting a little, aren't we?

  Doesn't make him

ED. like finger/prints

LUCY. Least he's never

MAN. You're right, he's not all **anti/helical**

LUCY. He is what he is.

MAN. You're right.

  Be good to see him again.

LUCY. Don't lie.

MAN. Alright, no, I don't feel the need to see him.

LUCY. Or any of our friends.

MAN. In time.

LUCY. Can't live as hermits, / can't

MAN. Just want to focus on **the helix, the lobe, the antitragus**,
  feels like enough / to be

LUCY. Focus? Do you have to concentrate particularly hard?

MAN. We haven't seen each other and you're the one I'm here to

LUCY. Are you staying then?

ED. the shape of the / helix

LUCY. You must have some kind of plan.

MAN. Not really.

LUCY. Money. Work. Must've thought about it.

MAN. I can look after myself.

LUCY. I'm sure you can.

ED. No one else on this planet has / that

LUCY. Who would you call? If you had to, is there anyone
    you'd call?

MAN. What do you mean, if there was an emergency or

LUCY. Anything, who would you call?

MAN. I'd

LUCY. Anyone.

MAN. I

　　Pause.

　　I looked it up and Robespierre declared France a republic.

LUCY. So what, you think he'd be a good person to call?

MAN. Is that how you say his name?

　　Robs-pierre? Robes-pierre?

　　anti-he-lical, anti-hell-ical

　　(*In a French accent.*) Robespierre.

　　anti-tray-gus, anti-traaa-gus, an-ti-tragus

LUCY. There's not going to be a quiz.

MAN. But I wanted to know.

> It could be Vendémiaire right now. Von-day-me-are-ray?
> Air-ray?

> That was the name they gave October, when they changed
> the calendar, when / they

LUCY. Turned the clock back to zero, I know.

MAN. Tried to start again, but it didn't work, / did it.

LUCY. Slicing each others' heads off a few years later.

MAN. Exactly. Ended in a whole load of bloodshed.

> I looked it up and I thought, **concha, the fossa**, I can't talk
> about the French Revolution. I don't know anything about it
> and it doesn't matter anyway, this isn't making me feel
> better, it's making me feel **helix**, it was just **antitragus**, I
> probably liked dinosaurs for a while, so what? Reading about
> it isn't going to bring me any closer to

> It doesn't matter now, it doesn't matter how you say
> Robespierre or Vendémiaire, so I'm done with the French
> Revolution.

LUCY. Well that's something.

> *Pause.*

MAN. I didn't think I'd hear from you.

LUCY. You weren't that boring.

> *He offers her the key.*

MAN. I wanted to give you this.

> LUCY *smiles.*

> What?

LUCY. Can't seem to give them away.

ED. The shape of the helix, that's the outer-/rim bit

LUCY. Ed gave his back too.

MAN. Oh. I'm sorry.

LUCY. Well actually, it is your fault, so

MAN. Here, take it Lucy.

It was generous of you, and it was a **concha**, I never thought you'd **fossa** me back like that, in fact, you weren't **antihelical** at all. But I did wait for you to leave, if I'm honest, before I let myself in, and I meant to be gone before you **lobe** but time got away from me when I **helix**. I didn't mean to scare you though, I just wanted to

LUCY. We fought about you.

MAN. If he's jealous, then he's got it wrong, I'm

LUCY. He's worried.

MAN. He sounds like a decent enough

LUCY. He brought me something but it wasn't his to give.

In fact, I think it probably belongs to you.

MAN. Me?

LUCY. Well

How am I going to

MAN. What is it?

LUCY. If I can't even

MAN. Lucy?

LUCY. How am I

Silence.

She shows him the plastic bag with the ear in it.

MAN *looks at it.*

MAN. Is that

Is that an ear?

LUCY *nods.*

So how can that belong to me, that's

LUCY. It's Jason's.

Silence.

I thought you were him.

I thought he was home.

I was properly shaking. Why?

Pause.

MAN. I want you to understand

LUCY. Did you think I wouldn't know?

MAN. What happened to Mum was payback for what I did. I set the wheels in motion with a single pig's head. I couldn't live with that.

LUCY. So he shot himself?

MAN. You can draw a direct, indelible line between a pig's head in a Hatfield mosque in nineteen ninety-three and Mum's death on a bus twelve years later. You might not be able to see it, but it's there.

I killed Mum.

LUCY. But he didn't.

Is that what he believed?

Silence.

MAN *takes the plastic bag from* LUCY. *He takes the ear out of the bag and holds it in the palm of his hand.*

He looks at it.

Ears are unique.

MAN *kisses it tenderly.*

Silence.

I don't even know your name.

Pause.

What's your name?

MAN. Frank.

LUCY. Frank?

Don't look like a Frank.

MAN. What do I look like?

LUCY. A Jason, actually.

MAN. Well it's Frank.

LUCY. Francis or

MAN. Frank.

LUCY. Why can't you be him?

Pause.

MAN. I wasn't trying to trick you.

LUCY. I thought you were him.

MAN. I'm sorry.

LUCY. I don't want an apology, I want you to be him, I want you / to

MAN. I only came here to, I don't know, blame you I guess. Accuse you. Make you feel bad, make myself feel better somehow, by making you feel bad.

But then when I saw you, and this place, it all felt familiar and I didn't want to go, I wanted to stay but I couldn't turn around then, could I, and tell you

You'd want nothing more to do with me, so I just, coward, just

LUCY. Stay.

Have his room. It's a single bed, and officially an office, but it's not like I ever actually work in / there

MAN. You only just learnt my name.

LUCY. You already have a key.

MAN. Which you should take back.

LUCY. Keep it.

MAN. You don't know me.

LUCY. Jason did.

MAN. I could be anyone Lucy, the police are still investigating what happened, you don't know / who

LUCY. You're Jason's family.

Aren't you?

MAN *nods*.

So am I.

MAN. I'm not Jason.

LUCY. Neither am I.

MAN. I don't want to be Jason, I just

LUCY. Neither do I.

See? We already have a lot in common.

Pause.

Stay tonight at least.

You don't have to move in, but I don't want to be alone in the house, maybe that old woman was right, maybe I should get a dog, I hate being alone and it's not the noises I hate, it's not the creaking Frank, it's the quiet, it's the, like I'm buried underground, no sound, nothing, it's suffocating, I can't breathe and I just want my mum, I just want her to hold me and tell me it'll be okay, but there's no one there Frank, no one.

MAN. There is.

He holds LUCY *as tight as he can*.

There is Lucy.

There is.

A Nick Hern Book

The Human Ear first published in Great Britain in 2015 as a paperback original by Nick Hern Books Limited, The Glasshouse, 49a Goldhawk Road, London W12 8QP in association with Paines Plough

The Human Ear copyright © 2015 Alexandra Wood

Alexandra Wood has asserted her moral right to be identified as the author of this work

Cover design by threaddesign.co.uk

Designed and typeset by Nick Hern Books, London
Printed in Great Britain by CPI Group (UK) Ltd

A CIP catalogue record for this book is available from the British Library

ISBN 978 1 84842 514 9

MIX
Paper from
responsible sources
FSC
www.fsc.org
FSC® C013604

www.nickhernbooks.co.uk

facebook.com/nickhernbooks

twitter.com/nickhernbooks